"No vestige of a beginning – no prospect of an end."

In 1788 a Scottish man conceived an extremely profound idea: the concept of geological time. Earth's history would never again be measured in thousands of years. But in millions. Conventional wisdom was about to be turned on its head. And soon a new science would make us look afresh at the world around us. A restless world on which we are its most recent passengers. Now you can discover the age of the Earth yourselves as we take you on a thrilling journey through the history of our planet.

"His study is so full of fossils and chemical apparatus of famous kinds, that there is hardly room to sit down."

A visitor to the man's home in Edinburgh, 1780.

Our Dynamic Earth is Scotland's most exciting visitor attraction. It's a journey of discovery that spans over 4,500 million years and every environment known to humanity. You'll experience everything from erupting volcanoes and ground-shaking earthquakes to freezing icebergs and tropical rainstorms.

This guide provides further insight into the forces that have shaped our planet and the species that have lived here through the ages. We hope that this guide will inspire you to find out more.

# contents

**Meet** the man who opened our eyes to the Earth as a machine.
**Discover** why the site of an extinct volcano provides the ideal window on our world and the way it works.

Think of the Earth as a colossal engine with an in-built repair mechanism. It takes heat from the inside and uses it to drive things on the outside. Changing the face of the landscape. It builds it up, it wears it down. The process is endless.

This thrilling theory was the brainchild of one man from Edinburgh, the 'Father of Modern Geology'. You can visit his natural laboratory. The city stands around it. Arthur's Seat is an extinct volcano. Our Dynamic Earth is designed to take you on an awesome voyage of discovery to witness the dramatic events which continue to shape our planet, making it unique throughout the universe.

# why Edinb

## Enter the Rock Detective

200 years ago Edinburgh bred a revolution. Hailed as 'The Enlightenment', it fuelled a renaissance in literary, scientific and artistic achievement, leading to the founding of The Royal Society of Edinburgh. Inspired by this 'hotbed of genius', was a man whose hobby would change history. James Hutton, doctor, farmer, chemist and businessman, dedicated his life to observing the relationships between different rocks across the Scottish countryside. Up until then most people accepted Archbishop Ussher's assertion that the Earth was 6,000 years old. But Hutton found evidence to the contrary.

## Shattering conclusion

Hutton argued that it takes an immense amount of time to turn sediments into rocks by squeezing and folding them under immense heat and pressure. So building mountains and eroding them again must then take millions of years. Thanks to his dogged detective work, the science of Geology was born. This changed everything. Particularly for Charles Darwin. He now had a credible time-frame against which to advance another ground-breaking theory. Natural Selection. Rocks are the key to the landscape of Edinburgh, too. But we have to look into a volcano to discover why.

## Born with a bang

Almost 350 million years ago Edinburgh lay near the Equator. Tell-tale signs of tropical climates are embedded in the limestone and coal around the city. And we have our own volcano. Arthur's Seat. Whinny Hill is the remnant of fiery lava flows. Lion's Head and the Lion's Haunch are what remains of its 'throat'. Salisbury Crags are the substructure where molten magma squeezed into the surrounding sediment. Hundreds of millions of years passed. Then came the Ice Ages. Peppered with rock, vast oceans of ice sandpapered the surface, grinding away until only the harder volcanic material remained upstanding. These are the hills and crags of today. That's why this site provides the perfect example of Nature shaping our environment the world over. But what else can it teach us?

## Worldwide think tank

Since Hutton and the 'Enlightenment', Edinburgh has become a major research centre, pooling its knowledge of the restless Earth with the global scientific community through its universities, museums and research institutes. It continues to examine what drives upheavals such as earthquakes and volcanic eruptions. It probes the impact of global warming on the vast ice fields of the Antarctic. It measures the scale of human activity on our fragile biodiversity. Our Dynamic Earth is a window on this world. A window to help you see far into the future.

Hutton confounds his critics.
Contemporary cartoon.

urgh?

Stare into the eye of a hurricane.
Clock the arrival of our planet's newest passengers.

Where's the coldest place on Earth? Answer: Vostock Station, Antarctica. Back in July 1983 it entered the record books with a chilling -89 degrees C. Colder than your freezer at home. Thanks to the World Meteorological Organisation sharing data accumulated by 10,000 land stations, 7,000 ships, swarms of aircraft, balloons and satellites, we can keep a wary eye on weather, around the clock. Armed with the microchip, the grandstand of space and global communications from TV to the Internet, we are beginning to shrink our world and sink with information. Yet less than 300 years ago, we groped in the dark .

# state of the

## A light in the dark

When James Hutton wanted evidence to support his theory of geological time, he had to resort to a horse and a sketchpad to get it. Thanks to his companion John Clark, his 3 year field trips into the Grampian mountains are meticulously preserved in watercolour. But he travelled light. No desk research to consult. No camera. And no television or website to share his inspiration with a grateful world. Up to this point, knowledge of the planet was limited. And in the 1760's when Hutton set out, this was a very big planet indeed. News of world events often took weeks or months to travel. Records of natural phenomena were few. In fact China provided the only instance of a concerted effort to catalogue floods, earthquakes and famine over generations. But Hutton's little sketchpad proved a searchlight for others to follow.

## Message in a bottle

Mary Anning, a 19th century fossil hunter from Dorset, gave us the first complete skeleton of a submarine dinosaur, Ichthyosaurus, encouraging others to systematically 'read the rocks'. By 1835 Britain had established the first national Geological Survey. Soon we began to interrogate almost everything. Meanwhile in Edinburgh, bottles of ooze from the seabed were yielding up the ocean's deepest secrets, following the voyage of the Challenger. But the jigsaw of Earth's story was riddled with gaps. No universal system of time. Uneven geographical input. Limited international co-operation. Would you believe that even by 1950 less than 10% of Africa had been mapped? Or 70% of the oceans? For the answers we had to leap into space and rely on microchips.

## Hell bubbles up

5.1 on the Richter scale. 15 tremors per hour. And by 8.32am on May 18 1980 Mount St Helens in Washington State, USA had erupted with the force of 500 Hiroshima bombs. Through a geological survey command post in Vancouver, Washington State monitoring the seismograms, forewarned was forearmed. Today, satellite technology, a global network of tracking stations, remote control sensors and the infinite capacity of the computer to collate and process huge amounts of data, put our restless Earth under the microscope. We can predict the weather, track a tornado, explore the ocean floor, measure energy consumption, even map the most densely populated areas across the globe. The nightime twinkling of our planet's surface speaks volumes to a satellite. But switch off the light for a moment and only 800 years ago all we had was a flat cloth. Mappa Mundi (map of the world) was peppered with abstract landscapes. Logic told you that since the information was on a flat surface, then the world it represented must be flat, too. Now our ability to see the 'big picture' is so far reaching, it has taken us back to the beginning of time.

The effects of an expanding population can be monitored from space.

# earth

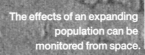
Remote sensors linked to computer networks track tornadoes and freak weather.

Seismograms provide an early warning of earthquake activity.

Time to get up. Time flies. Time's up. It seems we can't function for a second without it. See what I mean? We travel by it. Work by it. Eat by it. In fact, throughout history it's obsessed us to the point that we've devised all sorts of means to measure and manage it. From flowers to fire. You can't see or touch it but our bodies sense it. Tree rings record it. And the light from the stars shows us where it came from. Like it or not, we're all born 'clockwatchers'. So where did the bug begin?

# time mach

## The great dictator

If you can read hieroglyphics the Egyptians can tell you. They catalogued their pyramid building on stone tablets to record their slaves' daily progress. Very early on, man relied on the seasons to tell him when to hunt and farm. Then he tracked the position of the Sun in the sky to determine local time and set off to circumnavigate the unknown. But as life became more sophisticated, particularly with the Industrial Revolution, he was forced to record and manage it more efficiently. Down to the precious minute. After all, employees' pay was governed by the time they laboured. And then there was the question of the railways.

## Petal power

Starting with the shadow of the sundial, man's pursuit of time has been ingenious to say the least. Sand, water pressure, burning incense sticks and even flowers. A Swedish botanist, Carl Von Linnaeus, devised a flower clock in 1745. It worked on the principle of different plants opening and closing at different times of the day. The Dutch had already swung into action. In 1657, Christiaan Huygens gave us the world's first pendulum clock and our lives ticked over with accuracy and order. Almost. Up to the early 19th century people still relied on local time, setting their clocks by the Sun. But it's different depending on where you are. 6 minutes for every 1.5 degrees longitude. A journey of 470km in the same country was 25 minutes out. Havoc for a rail timetable. So in 1847 Greenwich Mean Time finally put us all on track. Today an atomic clock is accurate to one second in 3 million years. In spite of all this, Nature carries on regardless. Ask a butterfly.

## Flying time

When you disturb your natural routine and rob yourself of sleep, what happens? You experience a sensation called 'jet lag'. That's because we run on a natural rhythm of sleeping and waking, which is about 25 hours long. Other species depend on it to travel and reproduce. Take the Monarch butterfly, for instance. Every summer it migrates north to Canada, a distance of 3,000 kilometres. Even our cells are clockwatchers. As the years pass, they divide less to age us. So time dictates life and death on Earth, for everything. We can't stop it or travel through it. Only measure it. And there's only one tape measure long enough.

# ne

## Brief appearance

Written history charts thousands of years. Study the fossil record and you can measure right back to the Cambrian period and the earliest remains of life, 570 million years ago. But beyond that there's little to help you. Only the rock. And when Hutton learned to read it, the view was enormous. To give you an inkling, think back to the creation of our Earth and where you are now, in terms of a single day. Include every vestige of life there ever was, from the first bacteria. When do we turn up? You'll have to be patient. It's 2 seconds to midnight. To prove it means going back even further. To the very beginning. Back to a moment of pure energy. To the moment before time and a fireball, began.

Stand by for the greatest guided tour in the Universe.
Imagine holding galaxies in the palm of your hand.

Take a small coin like a 5p piece and put it in the palm of your hand. We'll return to it later.

Thanks to a 2.5 metre mirror orbiting 600 kilometres overhead, we've a window on the miracle of Creation. The Hubble space telescope can look back 11 billion years. Almost to the beginning. A few million short but the images we receive are enough to give you a ringside seat on the greatest light show ever. The cast is staggering. First there's Earth, within its galaxy of 100 billion stars we call the Milky Way. Now for the 'big picture'. Add another 100 billion galaxies and you have the entire Universe. Still expanding at the rate of 5,000 kilometres a second! Time to get back to your 5p.

# how it all s

## Savage birth

15 billion years ago, all matter and energy are concentrated into the size of that coin. And it's immensely hot. Before this, there was nothing. Now for a very, very Big Bang. Space and Time explode into being. A fraction of a second. Particles and radiation collide in a frenzy. Matter forms. Seconds tick and the temperature is dropping from billions to millions of degrees. Still 100 million times hotter than our sun's core. Tick. Tick. And the universe grows by a factor of 1,000. Protons and neutrons fuse to form atomic nuclei, Nature's building blocks. So far the entire Universe fills an area the size of our solar system. 60 seconds gone. The show's not over. It's still expanding. Now fast-forward half a million years. A blink of an eye to a cosmologist. Everything has cooled down. The fog of dust and gas is clearing. Gravity pulls matter into clumps. Galaxies are born.

## Cosmic drains

Powered by nuclear energy, the light from stars is the storybook which Hubble reads today. The bright blue ones end their short life spectacularly, exploding as a supernova to seed space with future generations of stars. Some stars collapse to form Black Holes. 500 million times the mass of our sun, their gravitational pull sucks in light and matter just like a drain, spewing out radiation in the form of ultra-bright beacons called quasars. But where does our light sparkle?

## Nuclear furnace

Billions of years ago, when the Universe was two thirds its present size, the Milky Way was formed. Over in one corner, gravity began pulling at a dense cloud of gas and cosmic dust, spinning them faster and faster together. Its core became dense and ferociously hot. Just like a nuclear furnace. Next a little yellow star was born. 1.4 million kilometres in diameter. This is our Sun. The remaining particles of this swirling cloud clumped together to become planets. Rocks formed the inner solar system of Mercury, Venus, Mars and Earth. Gas, ice and dust fused into Jupiter, Uranus, Neptune, Saturn and Pluto. And their neighbours are 63 moons and some dangerous debris, as you're about to discover.

tarted

**Discover** how many extraterrestrials arrive here every day.

**Calculate** how fast we're slowing down.

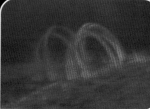

Gas flares from the sun scorch 483,000 kilometres into space.

One of one billion, this spiral galaxy is similar to our Milky Way.

The 'dirty snowballs' of space, the nucleus of a comet is a mass of ice and rock.

## Deep impact

On June 30 1908, Tunguska in Siberia had a visitor. In an ocean of flame it flattened forests, roasted reindeer and exploded with the force of a 12 megaton nuclear blast. That was an asteroid. 65 million years earlier, it's big brother, 9.6 kilometres wide, triggered a nuclear winter which wiped out the dinosaurs. Comets, meteorites and asteroids are the leftovers of Creation. However, thanks to our atmosphere, most uninvited guests burn up on entry. On average 2 get through every day. Estimates put our daily intake of micrometeorites at 8 tonnes, the equivalent of a medium sized truck. Though even the smallest can wreak havoc.

## Throbbing tempest

Before we head home, let's take a look at two influential neighbours. First the Sun. 5 billion years old and a very noisy gas ball. SOHO, Nasa's Solar & Heliospheric Observatory says so. It's been listening to the rumbles since 1995. Deep inside, hydrogen and helium gas at thermo-nuclear temperatures race to the surface to be bounced back, creating a constant throbbing motion at the core. Outside it is in constant eruption. Gas flares scorch 483,000 kilometres into space. Solar winds roar at 800 kilometres a second. Huge electromagnetic fields, the size of Earth, pepper its surface. Mammoth explosions trigger magnetic storms whose shockwaves can blackout power on our planet. Time to move on.

## Dead body

Only 385,000 kilometres to go now as we pass our nearest neighbour. Not a sound, either. No energy on the Moon. Or water. Just a stone dead body of dense rock. If it has a molten metallic core, Apollo's instruments failed to detect it. Yet without Earth, it wouldn't be there. Around 4 billion years ago, we had a close shave. Something the size of Mars passed uncomfortably close to Earth, sucking out huge chunks with its gravity. Chunks which re-fused into the satellite which orbits us today. It's been exerting its influence on us ever since. As our Earth rotates, the ocean on the side facing the Moon, bulges. Its gravitational pull dictates our tides.

## Third rock from the sun

Home at last! And what a colour. That's because 70% is water. Critical to our evolution, it moderates temperatures, erodes rocks, dissolves minerals and supports complex chemical reactions, some of which triggered single-celled life almost 3.8 billion years ago. At the core there's a solid iron nuclear reactor working at 4,000 degrees C. That's encased in a mantle of decaying radioactive elements, skinned by a fragile, shattered crust. From the inside out, heat drives our blue planet like an engine. For example, over millions of years, volcanic eruptions belched enough $CO_2$ (carbon dioxide) and $H_2O$ (water) to seed the atmosphere. But Earth is slowing down. 4 billion years ago our rotation calendered 875 days. Now it's 365. With the aid of atomic time, we should soon be able to predict when our number is up.

Discover why the Earth's surface isn't static like the Moon.
Guess where you could hide Mount Everest.

When you stare at the Moon what do you notice? It's pock-marked. Those giant craters are evidence of savage meteorite impact. And they never change. But our scars have healed. Why?

Our Earth is very much alive and renewing itself all the time. Widening oceans. Building vast mountain ranges. Even changing the climate for its inhabitants. In fact Scotland had a taste of the tropics 350 million years ago. Remember Arthur's Seat? But more of that later.

# the restles

## Letting off steam

So what exactly is going on beneath our feet? Recycling on an awesome scale. Let's imagine the Earth is an apple. Because in relation to its size, that's about the scale of the brittle crust that represents its skin. Inside at the core, radioactive decay generates temperatures almost as hot as the surface of the Sun. Cool and hard, the crust can only conduct so much internal energy away, so it relies on volcanoes as safety valves. And the energy under the surface moves the crust backwards and forwards, with spectacular results.

## Red hot conveyor belt

Oceans and continents lie on a patchwork quilt of slabs, called tectonic plates. These ride on currents of heat within the hot 'plastic' rock of the zone below called the mantle. Just like a conveyor belt. Only they're moving in different directions. Colliding. Tearing apart. Grinding past each other. This mammoth tug-of-war triggers earthquakes, ignites volcanoes and in one place in particular, adds millions of tonnes of new crust, widening the ocean floor. Iceland.

## Laboratory of fire

Did you know that there are many types of lava? The stuff that flows, like the water in Iceland's geysers, builds the ocean floor. It's called basalt. Where the crust splits along the sea bed, magma oozes up to cool and plug the gap. This widens the oceans and pushes continents further apart. In fact we're waving 'goodbye' to North America at the rate of 2.5 centimetres every year. Iceland is the peak of a giant underwater mountain range, called the mid-ocean ridge. Stretching for over 32,000 kilometres, this volcanic chain marks one of the boundaries between the giant tectonic plates. So if the Atlantic is growing at a finger-nail pace, why isn't the Earth getting bigger?

## Vanishing sea bed

The clue is in the age of the crust. Oceanic crust is ten times younger than the continents. Because the oceanic plate grows from the middle outwards, its edges are older. When it meets a continent, the heavier oceanic plate is forced underneath the lighter continental one, driving the ocean floor back down into the mantle. The process is called subduction, resulting in gigantic trenches along the edge of the ocean floor. Some as deep as 11 kilometres, could hide Mount Everest. And Nature's way of warning us? The earthquake.

# s earth

## Violent warning

Normally rock is elastic enough to absorb stress. But even a rubber band snaps when you stretch it too far. That's what happens when the edges of tectonic plates grind past each other, rupturing rock and shaking the ground. Japan understands the principle only too well. Thanks to a global network of listening devices called seismometers, we have an 'early warning' system. But as Nature is a balancing act and subduction destroys, what's responsible for its eternal land building programme?

Superheated steam bubbles cause sticky rivers of magma to explode in fountains of fire.  **17**

**Learn** how to make a volcano.
**Look** for the biggest sea of lava in Europe.

Stretching for 32,000 kilometres, the mid Altantic ridge is a volcanic submarine mountain range.

The continual collision of tectonic plates has stacked and folded the surface rock into mountains.

The giant cone and crater of one of nature's 'dragons'. 500 are active worldwide.

## Feeding the dragons

The clue to growing land lies in the deepest parts of the ocean. Remember those vast submarine trenches where old oceanic crust is recycled into the mantle by subduction? Well, as the surfaces of the two plates grind together, they melt, generating magma. Under pressure, this rises to the surface to feed coastal volcanoes, like the Andes in Chile. Think of them as 'rock factories' and you have the resources to build a continent. But unlike the ocean crust, their product is almost indestructible. And their secret is a sticky one.

## Exploding treacle

To better understand these lavas, imagine standing on the rim of Vesuvius, staring into the crater. Our gaze meets the magma coming up. Only this is like treacle. And it comes with a bang. Having punched its way through the continental plate below, this sticky magma has been concentrated, trapping superheated steam bubbles inside. As the magma bubbles up, pressure is released, causing the bubbles to expand and eventually explode. That's why it foams. (Shake a lemonade bottle before opening and you'll soon get the picture.) Much lighter and less dense than the mantle, continental crust stays on the surface forever.

## Collision course

Ever wondered what made an 8 kilometre high mountain called Everest? Buckling. That's what happens when an ocean disappears and two continents collide. Because they're made of the same lighter crust, they can't sink into the mantle. So they press on and on, bending, buckling and folding the rocks. India, once an island, smashed northwards into Asia, forming the Himalyas over 45 million years. It hasn't stopped, either.

## Rocky route map

We started by hinting at Scotland's link with the tropics. Due to the continual cycle of ocean creation and destruction, continents are propelled through different climatic belts. 700 million years ago, Scotland set out from the southern hemisphere. We've a route map of its voyage north. By reading the rocks, we have evidence of glacial environments, tropical swamps and deserts. But in all this time, why haven't all the continents stayed together?

## Ferocious hotspot

You'll find the Atlantic holds the answer. Let's go back 60 million years to when America and Europe were one. The plate it stood on was being pulled apart, East to West. Eventually it split, weakened by a hotspot under North West Scotland. A scorching plume of magma from the mantle beneath, gushed up. The rocks of Skye, Rhum, Mull and Ardnamurchan speak volumes.

## Off we go again

Don't be too complacent. That hotspot is still at work, under the Atlantic mid-ocean ridge. At 200 degrees C hotter than the rest of the mantle, it's been splitting Iceland apart since even before the days of the Vikings. Locals can expect a sizeable eruption every five or six years. Volcanoes sprout along the coast as the ocean floor continues to spread. Where will it end? Who knows?

Fly over a gigantic glacier in a thrilling helicopter ride.

Learn how a holidaymaker from Switzerland gave us the clue to the face of Scotland.

At the risk of having your feet singed

by a torrent of lava, you saw how the Earth

can build up land. Now it's time to stand on the

top of a mountain to watch it get worn down again.

# shaping th

## Awesome destruction

Just as heat drives volcanoes and tectonic plates, weather is an engine, too. It helps nature to complete a continuous process of renewal. With a nudge from gravity, the forces of wind, ice and water can take a mountain apart, bit by bit, to send it all the way back to the ocean as fine grains of sand. We promised you a bird's eye view of how our landscape was shaped, particularly by ice. You've taken a breathtaking journey down a survivor of the last great Ice Age, a giant glacier, as it snaked its way relentlessly to the sea. But let's come down to earth for a moment.

## Eating rock

So how exactly does weather help bring down something as formidable as a mountain or a cliff face? It starts by attacking the rock. By breaking it down into fragments, it can move it almost anywhere. We owe some of the coastline of Norfolk to the erosion of Norway's mountains. A number of forces help the process along. Waves pounding the coast are a prime example. Violent changes in temperature burst rock by expansion and contraction. Granite and limestone literally rot because they're eaten away

## Sand from the sky

Did you know that thanks to the wind, Hawaii is home to dust from Central Asia, 11,000 kilometres away? Next time you handle a pebble, just remember that the smoother it is, the further it's travelled. Rivers carry everything from boulders, to silt and clay down to the sea. Then the coast takes over. Steered by currents and tides, the debris forms beaches or is washed far out to sea. But the most spectacular conveyor belt of all is ice. It can move rocks marathon distances. And thanks to a Swiss naturalist, we now know why Scotland looks the way it does today.

## Shattering deduction

Up until 1837 no-one had a clue that ice had shaped Scotland's landscape. Not until Louis Agassiz came here for a holiday. Having seen how a titanic glacier could shape the valleys of Switzerland, he instantly recognised the tell-tale scars on our rocky terrain. Only ice, he deduced, could leave such shattering clues. You can see the process happening in Switzerland, today. If this was the case, he asserted, then most of northern Europe must have been covered by glaciers. The time had come to piece the puzzle of

e surface

A survivor of the last Ice Age, this glacier has been carving its way through the landscape for 2 million years.

**Follow** the path of a mountain as it turns to mud.
**See** how Nature's sandpaper carved out the face of Edinburgh.

To complete the picture, we have to go back 2 million years. To the beginning of the last Ice Age. Or rather the one that we're living on the edge of today. Back then vast ice sheets several kilometres thick covered most of the northern hemisphere. Britain was entombed as far as the south of England. During this time, the climate see-sawed between intense cold and milder periods. Then what happened?

Rock locked inside the ice sheet makes this one of the toughest abrasives on Earth.

## Mightiest sandpaper on Earth

These swings in temperature caused the vast skin of ice blanketing almost 30% of the planet, to shrink and grow, moving it backwards and forwards across the continents. Even then, what remained in the valleys was hundreds of metres thick. Locked inside and underneath, millions of rock fragments acted like an abrasive. Add the colossal weight of the ice sheet bearing down on the ground beneath to the driving force of gravity and you have Nature's answer to sandpaper. When the ice finally retreats, its vigorous handiwork reveals itself in the familiar U-shaped valleys, scarred rock formations and hummocky hills that are Scotland today.

## Trail of a juggernaut

As you swept over that mammoth glacier, did you notice any of its characteristic features? Pure as driven snow at the mountain tops, it became increasingly stained on its downward journey. Those distinctive dark bands are the tell-tale signs of rock debris. As well as acting like sandpaper, a glacier is a conveyor belt, too. It takes huge amounts of rock from the mountain summit all the way to the valley floor, dumping it along the way to re-shape the landscape. Many distinct features result. And one is an Edinburgh landmark. A crag and tail is what happens when ice meets a barrier. Scouring its way around the obstinate rock, it hews out the shape we recognise today. You can see its handiwork within sight of Our Dynamic Earth in the ridge descending from the Castle to the Palace of Holyrood House.

## Giant's footprints

Almost 18,000 years ago the ice sheets drew back. Their titanic scouring action left features common to all glaciated landscapes. Lake-filled craters called Corries. Valley sides etched into smooth U-shapes. At its snout, where the glacier's energy has finally been consumed, debris marks the limit of its progress. Now here's where the meltwater takes over.

## Water sculpture

Carrying the rock relentlessly on towards the sea, the river torrents carve out deep V-shaped gullies, while sifting and depositing sand and gravel. Beyond the hills the water slows, dumping sediment and causing rivers to meander like snakes. By now only the finest rock particles will reach the sea. Here the sediment will build new land, a delta, at the river's mouth or disappear with the tide to line the ocean floor. But the cycle isn't over by any means. As the process is endless, layer upon layer of sediment on the sea bed will compress it all back together again. As rock.

The scouring action of a glacier creates a distinctive steep-sided valley.

At its snout, the glacier dumps rock fragments all the way from the mountain summit.

**Stare** into the 'soup' of life. **Trace** your earliest ancestors. **Discover** what killed off the dinosaurs.

3.8 billion years ago this planet was invaded. The force was modest in comparison to the Big Bang. A few thousandths of a millimetre in size. Yet its impact was equally colossal. How's this for a CV? Versatile, tenacious and indestructible. It survived ice ages and nuclear winters. Unperturbed it went on to systematically transform the face of the planet to what we recognise today. Beginning with its atmosphere. If that sounds like a virus, you're close. It's life!

# casualties

## Bubbling broth

Preserved in the rock of southern Africa are what looks like rice grains. Identical in shape to bacteria living today, these microscopic organisms are the oldest forms of life. And they thrived in a bubbling broth similar to the scalding hot springs of Yellowstone Park in North America. Except that this primeval soup was stoked by a lethal atmosphere of hydrogen, ammonia, carbon dioxide and methane. Bathed in scorching ultraviolet rays. Bombarded with electrical storms. And cocooned in the perfect incubator, water. Next came DNA and life began to multiply.

## Submarine explosion

Deep in the sediment within the oceans, algae began breathing life into our atmosphere. They fed off carbon dioxide and replaced it with oxygen. Left to simmer for another 3 billion years, the recipe exploded with frenzied activity. Marine creatures with hard parts appeared. Shells, bones and teeth evolved to aid survival. However, even the body armour of a Trilobite couldn't deter Anomalocaris. This shrimp-like invertebrate, the size of a puppy, ripped them apart with the aid of its tentacles. Uninhibited, other species proliferated in vast submarine communities. Until calamity struck. 440 million years ago an Ice Age wiped the slate. Almost. Struggling to survive, life fought back with hardier new species and brought the battle out of the water.

## Invasion force

Primitive moss-like plants were the first to colonise the land, followed by miniature forests a metre high. And into this tropical habitat crept tiny creatures. Canada's Joggins Fossil Forest crawls with their remains. But disaster struck again. Continents collided causing sea levels to fall. Radical climate change and the fight for space did the rest. 250 million years ago life stumbled towards extinction. Once again evolution came to the rescue. In a harshly competitive environment, size mattered. Enter the dinosaur and 74 million years ago Tyrannosaurus Rex forced evolution on his prey. Claws to burrow and hide. Camouflage. But deep in space something was about to nudge things further.

## Dinosaur deathbed

In Mexico there's a buried meteorite crater 177 kilometres in diameter. 65 million years ago this visitor probably detonated the nuclear winter which wiped out the dinosaurs. Challenged by lack of food, shelter and warmth, their natural successor came prepared. Fur as insulation and a warm-blooded biology. Shrew-like mammals began to fill the dinosaur's footprints. In another 62 million years, man would be hard on their heels. Today we thrust change on nature. We clone sheep and genetically alter food. But our sophisticated ecosystem is still vulnerable. Faced with a global catastrophe, how well could we adapt?

# & survivors

Watch how space is giving us lessons in good behaviour.
Discover why an artificial environment is shaping the natural world.

By the time you've read this chapter, there'll be 300 new voices to compete with your own. All demanding more. That's 27 every 10 seconds. Almost a quarter of a million every day of the year. Estimates are that the world's population has doubled since 1960. Today it's almost 6 billion. But why worry, there's plenty of room on the rock. The challenge isn't so much the numbers. It's what's happening to our Earth to support them.

# the human

## Family album

With nightime satellite imaging, we can take stock of our progress. The twinkling lights of civilisation provide illuminating evidence of settlement, population density and energy consumption, highlighting our prospects for the future. And the limitations. Here's a body that's been running itself for almost 4.5 billion years. Then, in the blink of a geological eye, one passenger starts to change things. This species, one of one hundred million, needs more of everything. Water. Food. Shelter. Energy. And answers. That's why it's never happy with Nature's menu. It strives to be in control. Consequently the human animal has evolved its own ecosystem which is already encroaching on its neighbours. So what's got into us in the last 2 million years? One man found the answers in the teeth of a baby.

## Dr Dart's baby

In 1924 in Southern Africa near the Equator, anatomist Raymond Dart first found our earliest ancestor. He christened it *Australopithecus* because the skull of this 2 million year old child told him an extraordinary story. It ate meat and stood upright. Here was a creature which foraged for food with its hands not its mouth and relied on tools to catch it. A mammal with a brain weighing 0.681 kilos was beginning to make its own rules. And a million years later, he was showing signs of invention.

Evidence in China has a descendant, Peking Man, using fire. By the time of Neanderthal Man, our on-board computer had increased capacity and doubled in weight. The equivalent of *Homo sapiens* today. Things began to accelerate. Numbers grew rapidly. Hunting couldn't support a growing population. Able to predict the result of his actions, it was move or starve. And we did – over prodigious distances. 400,000 years ago we migrated from Africa to Europe. Then someone discovered wheat and life went into overdrive.

## City of wheat

Jericho was the forerunner of the 'megalopolis'. Today that means a 'million person city' and currently there's 41 bursting with 5 million inhabitants. Expect another 23 by 2015. Back in 6000 BC, Jericho was the earliest example of a major agricultural settlement. We'd ceased being nomads. Agriculture proved the first real civilising influence and from here on, man began to shape his environment. This walled city spelled the birth of urban living and to sustain it our demands on the land grew. By 5500 BC irrigation was boosting crop yield. The plough made its mark in 3000 BC and we began to dictate our future. We were free to be artists, craftsmen, merchants and builders. Two thousand years ago, the relatives of baby *Australopithecus* had mushroomed to 300 million.

Language, art and the global satellite, make us the most versatile communicator of all the species.

In 1969 the Moon finally fell prey to our natural urge to explore.

# animal

## Precious plot

Do you realise that we have a lot in common with a chimp? 99% of our genes, in fact. They can use tools, too. And solve problems. But only simple ones. What makes us unique, is our capacity for imagination, reason, invention and communication. Listen to Mozart or Beethoven and you'll soon get the picture. We're the only species that leaves traces of our unique gifts. Tools, transport, buildings, jewellery, and pottery. And ultimately, pollution. Which is why space can help us keep our feet on the ground. We can keep a wary eye on what we're doing. We're the only species with the brainpower, remember. And one further thought. Evolution. You've come a long way from *Australopithecus*. But Darwin has revealed that nothing escapes its relentless appetite. And one day, another creature could be scrutinising the skull of a long lost city dweller. *Homo sapiens*.

**Sink** beneath the waves in a deep sea submersible.
**Follow** the chain reaction of an underwater earthquake.

Before you take the plunge, the view from NASA's space probe Galileo helps with the 'big picture'. As far as we know, our Blue Planet is the only one in our solar system cradled in life-giving water. It covers 70% of the surface. Without it, life would be intolerable. It's a thermostat, a waste disposal unit, a worldwide highway, a playground and a food factory. But when currents change direction, offspring like El Nino can wreak havoc globally.

# the ocean

## Alien underworld

As we're beginning to discover, the oceans are home to minnows and monsters. Blink and you'd miss all 8mm of the dwarf goby fish, while an encounter with a sperm whale would be like stopping a 50 tonne truck. Yet we know less about this crowded neighbourhood than we do about the surface of Mars. Only 1% of the deep sea floor. In 1872 the science of oceanography began. Back then no-one believed there was life below 33 fathoms. 3 years later, HMS Challenger returned with evidence in its nets which gave scientists in Edinburgh enough to fill 50 text books. Today titanium alloy submersibles, like the ones that found the Titanic, have opened our eyes to an alien underworld.

## Killer wave

4 kilometres down lies a floor of peaks and troughs. Volcanic mountain ranges tower over the sea floor. Near the Mariana Islands in the Pacific, is the deepest point on Earth. An 11 kilometre abyss. Balance 48 jumbo jets on your head and you've some idea of the pressure down there. Meanwhile, volcanic islands are growing. In 10,000 years a new neighbour will surface to join the Hawaiian

chain. However, all this disturbance and related earthquakes, has a habit of unleashing one of man's deadliest enemies. A Tsunami (great harbour wave) can grow to a record 92 metres. At speeds of 965 kilometres an hour, one devasted the Japanese Ryuku Islands in 1971 and another drowned 36,000 people near Krakatoa in 1883. Yet despite such calamities we depend on the oceans to survive. Why?

## Swirling mass

Try thinking of them as a giant blue conveyor belt. It needs to be. We're moving 1.4 billion cubic kilometres of the planet's salt water. What powers it up is the pumping action of heat and salt. Cold, salt-rich and consequently dense surface water sinks, displacing deep water to the surface. And the cycle begins. The 'start button' is friction. Wind pushes the surface water, creating waves and they're steered by the Earth's rotation. One of the strongest currents, the Gulf Stream, moves heat from the Caribbean into the North Atlantic bringing moist, warm air and a balanced climate to Europe. And we can track these movements, too. With shoes.

S

## Treasured castaways

Beachcombers in British Columbia and Oregon couldn't believe
their luck. Free Nike trainers.
Hundreds came ashore. 12 months earlier, 60,000
had spilled overboard in a Pacific storm in
1990. Plotting the findings by computer,
scientists successfully predicted their
route. Next stop Japan, the Phillipines
and back to North America again
by 1997. But now and again
currents can shift into reverse.
Then all hell breaks loose.

## Vicious cycle

In September 1997 Mexico hit the headlines. Packed with more energy than a million Hiroshima bombs, Hurricane Linda lashed its coast at 298 kph. 8 months later, El Nino had left a litany of disaster from Peru to Australia. Flood, drought, forest fires and death. Its source was a pool of warm seawater the size of Canada, off the coast of Papua New Guinea. Triggered by a change in air pressure, the Pacific currents changed direction and blocked the rise of cooler waters from the deep. This is significant when you realise that the ocean is a sandwich.

## Grub's up

Oceans aren't the same all the way through. The top layer is warm water nourished by the sun. Nearly 200 metres down beyond a boundary called a thermocline, it's cold. Almost 0 degrees C. The lower you go, density increases with the salt content. On the blackness of the ocean floor, the remains of plants and microscopic organisms congeal in a nutrient rich stew. All it needs is a stir called an Upwelling. That's what happens when deep cold water currents collide with land. The impact sucks the 'fertiliser' to the surface to replenish the food chain. And the banquet begins.

## Feast or famine?

Here's the menu for Scottish coastal waters. Plankton for herring. Herring for cod. Cod for seals. And succulent seal for the discerning killer whale. Simple, efficient and reliable. Until we come along with a million floating factories and an insatiable appetite. With the fervour of a piranha shoal, global fishing is devouring links in the food chain that sustain marine life. Faster than nature can re-stock.

## Black smokers

Nourished by light, you'll encounter 80% of marine life close to the surface. That's where the food is. Below 900 metres lies a graveyard for scavengers. Only the giant sperm whale crosses this chilling frontier. So it came as a shock to scientists in the depths of the Pacific in 1979, when a cloud of hot water raced up to meet them. At 350 degrees C, superheated plumes of black smoke melted their submersible's external thermometer. Cool sea water was being leeched through volcanic rock which recycled it as a hot, chemical-rich geyser. But what came next, proved stunning. The darkness was teeming with life. 'Black Smokers' are a grazing ground for clams, shrimps and gigantic tube worms over 2 metres long.

## Underwater metropolis

Who made the biggest structure on Earth? Australia's Great Barrier Reef is testimony to the collective endeavour of coral. 350 species of this minute organism populate the world's largest coral reef. 2,000 kilometres of it. Thanks to them it's home to countless marine creatures from crustaceans to exotic fish. But of all the ocean's habitats, from the Deep to the Temperate and the Tropics, the Polar Seas may prove the most significant. Locked in the

The best way to acclimatise to the Poles is to start at home. In your kitchen. Open the fridge and look in the freezer. Ice is exactly the same stuff that distinguishes this environment. Except that out there it's accompanied by rumbling and crashing. The sound of calving as it breaks off. But apart from one thing in common, these regions are 'poles apart'. The Arctic is an ocean surrounded by land, whereas the Antarctic is land surrounded by ocean. The Antarctic is the fifth largest continent. Bigger than Europe or Australia. You'll find more ice there, too. As well as penguins. But no polar bears. In contrast the Arctic is a lot more hospitable. Inuits live there. But what makes these regions so different?

# the polar r

## Poles apart

Apart from Greenland and the mountainous margins of Eurasia and North America, the Arctic Ocean consists almost entirely of sea ice. Because it's thin and less dense than water, it floats. That's why nuclear submarines can pass beneath it on routine patrols. Without roots it is constantly on the move and vulnerable to the flexing motion of the ocean beneath. The Antarctic, by contrast, is almost 14 million square kilometres of mountainous terrain smothered under a blanket of ice 4 km thick. Only the tips of the mountains can breathe. Across the ice cap, monumental glaciers, fed by snow, grind their way relentlessly towards the sea. As you might expect, the volume of ice here is much greater than the Arctic. In fact Antarctica contains more than two thirds of the world's fresh water.

## Weeks to live

Out here on the edge of the world, each species has developed its own remarkable survival code. Penguins live off their body fat. Birds on the Arctic Tundra simply migrate to warmer climes. But in the Antarctic, life teems beneath the sea. 30 million years breeds cold water experts. Fish have evolved a 'chemical antifreeze'. Jellyfish, krill and squid feed on the nutrient-rich waters. Plants have to work fast out here. Their saviour is light. But with Summer compressed into weeks rather than months, the cycle of life, death and reproduction goes into overdrive. They harvest as much energy from the light as possible. Stems become trunks to keep out the cold. Deserts of ice bloom into carpets of colour. Darkness descends. White reigns again.

## Deserts of life

Both poles are rationed to small amounts of the Sun's energy. Summers are short, winters long. Even a summer's day in the Antarctic can be 30-below-zero. Deserts of ice see less than 20 centimetres of snowfall in a year, although the mountainous Antarctic sees more. Here light dictates growth. Only the most adaptable plants and animals can hope to survive. And then only at the margins. To the penguins, seals and whales of the Antarctic, home means the shoreline and surrounding marine oceans. At the Arctic, however, life is afloat. Roaming its sea ice is the Polar bear, leaving the wolf, reindeer and caribou to stalk the fringeing land areas which merge into the Tundra. But are they alone?

# egions

Hundreds of tonnes of ice shatter and break off in the relentless process of calving.

Nuclear submarines regularly pass under the sea ice of the Arctic Ocean.

The Polar Bears forage for food on the sea ice of the Arctic.

With only weeks to bloom, the life cycle of Arctic plants goes into 'overdrive'.

## Disappearing wilderness

So in the face of such hostility, why on earth would we go to the Antarctic? Perhaps because it still is the last great wilderness. 10,000 tourists a year would agree. However, the real magnet is knowledge. With all this ice, the Antarctic represents the biggest time capsule on the planet. So valuable, in fact, that as a natural laboratory, it has been protected by international treaty since 1959. Each season, 1,000 scientists representing 23 nations live and work here on 40 permanent bases. But what exactly are they looking for?

## Secrets of an invisible lake

Far beneath the surface of Antarctica's awesome wilderness, 3,500 metres down, lies a lake. No-one's seen it yet but Lake Vostock is estimated to be the size of Lake Ontario in Canada. So far, borings using a remote controlled probe to avoid pollution, have reached to within 150 metres. Could a whole new range of microbiology be waiting?

## Ice cube test

The Poles affect ocean temperature. As giant ice cubes, they release vast quantities of cold water into the ocean currents. But don't be alarmed. If the sea-ice of the Arctic melted, water levels wouldn't rise and drown continents. You can test it by observing an ice cube in a glass of water. When it melts, the level doesn't rise because the cube simply displaces its own volume. However, the land ice at the Antarctic is a different matter. But scientists believe that if temperatures rise, the dangers are still centuries away. The real concern comes from the thermal expansion of the oceans themselves. And a rise in the Earth's overall temperature will decide that. So how real is such a threat and where could it come from?

## Hot spot

The answer lies in the skies above Antartica. A breach in our atmosphere's ozone layer. By upsetting the delicate balance of the 'Greenhouse Effect', which keeps our planet at an equable warm temperature, increased exposure to the Sun's radiation could cause overall surface temperatures to rise. With destructive results. As the most sensitive spot on the planet, Antarctica could prove to be the best 'barometer' of this phenomenon. Especially when we dig deep into the ice cap.

## Crystal Bubbles

For James Hutton, rocks spoke volumes. He said, 'the past is the key to the future'. But within the ice of Greenland and the Antarctic, tiny bubbles of atmospheric gas trapped in the ice, are telling scientists about trends in temperature, too. Millions of years ago. With the aid of computers, they can trace fluctuations in the Earth's temperatures through the history of the polar ice caps. Matched against current changes induced by man, we can attempt to predict what the long term future holds.

Follow the trail of Life's 'crush hour'.
Discover why humans make themselves the most vulnerable species on the planet.

Have you any idea how many neighbours you have on the planet? Try 100 million species. Insects alone outnumber us by nearly a million to one. But because energy dictates life, living room is restricted. You'll find half of all the terrestrial species crammed into just 2% of our Earth's surface. So where is everybody else? To find them you have to cross five distinct habitats.

# journey of

## Population explosion

At the wilderness of the Poles, it's difficult to imagine a planet teeming with vitality. Starved of light and energy, few species of plant or animal life can survive. Journey south, however, from Tundra to Tropics and after 5,000 kilometres you'll hit Nature's 'crush hour'. Between these two points, warmth and water regulate life like a tap, flooding the Equator in spectacular biodiversity. Head south from the Arctic and solar energy defines the seasons as winter, spring, summer and autumn. Closer to the Equator, the climate is simply wet or dry. To appreciate these differences, we first have to cross the ArcticTundra.

## Flying fury

Peppered with lakes, this vast black marshy plain blankets constantly frozen ground called permafrost. In these extremes, Arctic poppies can expect only 60 days of bloom. This is the land of the reindeer and in the summer, a flying plague. A bite from a Tundra mosquito makes their tropical relatives seem playful. Beyond lies the Taiga. Vast coniferous forests that cloak North America and Eurasia, with Siberia the largest of all. This is the feeding ground of the wolf and brown bear.

## Recipe for heaven

Now we enter the Temperate zone, home to the forests and grasslands of the mid-latitudes. Here oceans and mountains shape distinct climatic variations and seed the fertile brown soils of agriculture. Fringed by the Mediterranean with its hot dry summers and warm wet winters, the European continent enjoys a long growing season. Consequently this part of the Earth's surface is one place on the planet whose natural habitat has been significantly affected by man. Vast forests have fallen to the farmer since the Middle Ages.

## Danger zone

Since the Industrial Revolution, urban living has been forcing plants and animals to compete for nature's finite resources. Today nearly half the world's population of 6 billion live in towns. By 2025 the UN predict 60%. And its appetite is voracious. To sustain its growth, we even turn precious water into sand. The Aral Sea in the former Soviet Union, is a prime example. By diverting its feeder rivers for intensive farming, an inland sea is drying up. And with it, the wildlife. But an urban species is a vulnerable species. Put Edinburgh in the path of that Tunguska asteroid you read about earlier and you soon get the picture.

Four distinct seasons
shape the Temperate
forests and grasslands
of the mid latitudes.

Africa's Savanna,
represents one
fifth of the world's
grasslands.

# contrasts

## Battle for supper

Next stop the Desert. A third of the Earth's surface and one of
the driest places on the planet. Ferociously hot days, bitterly cold
nights. Rainfall here is unpredictable and precious. Less than
25cm a year. Plants hoard water deep within their tissues. Then
flash floods drown everything in sight. At almost 6 million square
kilometres, the Sahara is by far the largest. In the cool of night,
life battles for food. Spiders, scorpions and lizards battle over a
meagre menu of insects, eggs and the occasional fruit. But next
door, the ground is covered in food. And fire helps it grow.

Half the world's
population,
3 billion people,
live in towns.

## Upside down trees

Across Africa, you'll find one fifth of the world's grassland.Some
of it as tall as an elephant. This is the Tropical Savanna. And here
you'll encounter the oldest tree in the world. One of life's natural
survivors, the Baobab or Upside Down tree can live for thousands
of years. Its 10 metre diameter trunk is fire resistant and its water
storing capacity is legendary. Long dry summers breed fire
but each scorching acts like a fertilser, raising the grass up in
abundance. No scramble here. Equal shares for all. Zebras munch
from the top stems. Wildebeest guzzle the middle. Gazelles chomp
the bottom, leaving bushes for the Dik-diks and tree leaves for
the Giraffe. From Tundra to Tropics, life struggles for resources
to survive. But at the crush of the Equator, the banquet begins in
earnest as you're about to discover.

On the Tundra's
snowy wastes,
the Inuit heard
their reindeer.

Listen to the electric hum of insect life.

Do you realise that the one place on earth we take for granted is the one place where life thrives most rapidly? And with our help it's vanishing. We're talking of the world's biggest 'hothouse'. One that spans four continents and teems with life. Imagine rubbing shoulders with 60,000 different species of plant and animal life, in an area the size of a soccer pitch. This is a place of extremes. Ferns are as tall as trees. Reptiles fly. Bamboo shoots up by 23 centimetres a day. And we use the forest's treasures everyday. Look around your home. Where do you think those mahogany doors, toiletries, detergents, medicines and kitchen spices come from? Even chewing gum. So can we afford to lose it? For the answer, we need to climb three storeys.

# the tropica

## Triple decker incubator

Right around the globe, the tropics are a warm, wet climatic band that spans Africa, Asia, Australia and South America. There you'll find the tropical rain forests. South America's Amazon, by far the largest at 6 million square kilometres, is home to one fifth of the world's birds and plants. 143 primitive tribes live there, too. And they're all tenants of a uniquely similar environment the world over. Not 'jungle' in the way you might expect. This is more like a three storey greenhouse with vast communities sharing very different environments the higher you climb. On one level, some of its residents will kill for a glimpse of the light.

## Sunshine killers

Level one is the forest floor. A maze of tuberous tree roots, ferns and fallen branches. It's very still, sultry and dark down here. That's because 15 metres overhead there's a giant 'sponge' almost 7 metres thick, blocking your view. This is the canopy. Up here the foliage is so dense it soaks up sunlight and rainfall. Which is why some plants will do anything to stay there. Climbers known as lianas, coil their aerial roots around the tree trunk to the security of the floor below. Some, like the Strangler fig, eventually choke their host to death by selfishly blocking out its light. But this doesn't inhibit Emergents.

## Launchpad for lunch

Punching their way through the dense canopy, tower straight-trunked monsters. Usually Emergent trees can reach 45 metres but in the Penang forest in Malaysia, there's a record-breaker, almost twice this size. With such supernatural growth, perhaps it's no wonder that the natives believe spirits live in the treetops. If they do, they share it with a screeching metropolis of monkeys and birds. In Central and South America, these wooden skyscrapers are the perfect launchpad for one of the world's largest eagles, the Harpy. From its lofty perch it can swoop down through the canopy to snatch a sloth off a branch for lunch. At these dizzy heights the trees are equally resourceful. Leaves are waxed to hoard the daily downpour, as you're about to discover.

rainforest

Earth's biggest 3 storey greenhouse, breeds trees up to 90 metres high.   39

Experience a heart-stopping jungle thunderstorm.
Meet beetles the size of mice.

**This South East Asian Orang-Utan is losing his home to forest clearance at the rate of 40 hectares a minute.**

## Clockwork deluge

You can almost set your watch by this climate. Lights off at 6pm prompt. Temperatures rarely fall below a constant 25 degrees C. And there's no dry season, except in the monsoon forests of Asia. At altitudes of 1,000 metres, where the lowland forest becomes a Montane forest, a heavy mist constantly blankets the treetops. Everything drips. But come 9am, the mist vanishes down below so life can look forward to a soaking. On cue at 4pm and 4am everyday, down come the biggest raindrops in the world. Upping rainfall levels to an annual 1,500mm. With such a reliable plumbing system, everyone benefits, from the crowds in the canopy to the denizens of the dark far below. But who are they?

## Skyscraper ants & miracle lizards

The best way to find out is to drop in on them, just like one of these watery 'golfballs'. First stop, treetop. Scorched by the sun, it's hotter and drier than anywhere in the forest. Here leaf-eating monkeys graze. Alongside macaws, snakes and fireflies. Next stop, the canopy. A gallery teeming with tree frogs, anteaters, stick insects, fruit bats, hummingbirds and monkeys. Get set for a cushioned landing on the litter of the forest floor. Among the ferns, you'd be hard put to see anything. This is the camouflaged domain of beetles the size of mice, termites and spiders. Ants nest in climbing plants all the way back up into the skyscraper canopy. Down by the river, the mangrove swamps are awash with snakes and amphibians. One reptile in Central America can walk on water using its tail as a balance. And what do you think they call this miracle worker? Jesus Christ.

## Living litter

You've heard of the phrase, 'manna from heaven', well the rain forest proves it. What dies in the skies ends up as compost. And it crawls. Unlike urban civilisation, here litter doesn't hang about. Dead leaves and creatures falling from above are rapidly absorbed into the shallow topsoil for recycling. Inside this layer, no deeper than the height of a boot, legions of worms, insects and bacteria join ranks for reprocessing debris into nutrients for themselves and the vegetation above. But this succulent skin is fragile. Exposure will scatter it to the winds. And that's only the beginning.

## Lost laboratory

Do you know the quickest way to kill a rain forest? Drive a road into its heart. It's as lethal as a dagger. In go the loggers and miners. Next come the farmers. Then stand back and watch the vegetation and its inhabitants all wilt away. Forever. That's the prospect. But in return for all its material resources what are we sacrificing? Control of our destiny. Apart from refreshing the atmosphere with oxygen and influencing rainfall, these giant hothouses are laboratories of life. Life that holds the key to 100 million years of evolution. Yet we've only catalogued a fraction of their residents. And if we keep on going that'll be the sum of our knowledge of a vanishing ecosystem. Then what?

Breeding time for a South East Asian Atlas moth, one of thousands of species packed into the biggest hothouse on the planet.

'Lunch is up for the brood of a central American Quetzal.

The striking colours of a Brazilian Katydid send a 'keep your distance' message to predators.

What do you have in common with a mite? You're both passengers and the ride is alive. That's what the 'rock detective', James Hutton concluded over 200 years ago, when he conceived the idea of 'geological time'. However, after 40 pages of colliding continents, exploding treacle and El Nino, you'd be forgiven for believing that chaos reigns. To put things in perspective, let's imagine you're a mite for a moment. About a quarter the size of the full stop you're heading for. *Demodex follicorum* to be precise. Now climb aboard an eyelash and all will come clear in the blink of an eye.

# the showd

## Body beast

Humans host their own ecosystems, just like the Tundra and the Tropics. In fact, your 1.7 metres of skin is home to roughly as many bacteria as there are people in the USA. They're feeding on your cells right now. But let's not ruin a lifelong attachment. Perched on an eyelash, a human sneeze is awesome. An earthquake and a blizzard, all in one. A teardrop becomes a flood of biblical proportions. Dry skin a drought. And we'll leave a boil to your imagination. Like *Demodex*, you are hitching a ride on a living organism. Just like the human body, the Earth is constantly regenerating and repairing itself. The hazards that make life seem like a rollercoaster, are simply the physical manifestations of a body at work. It's only when they touch us that events become catastrophies.

## Ferocious steamroller

The residents of the Caribbean have long accepted that danger comes with the territory when living off the bounty of fertile volcanic soil. On May 8 1902 the clock stopped at 7.52am for the citizens of St Pierre on the thriving French colony of Martinique. In 2 minutes a dense super-heated cloud of gas steamrollered down Mont Pelee to consume almost the entire population of 30,000 people. 2 survived. Today there are over 500 active

those near people. On average, 168 major disasters from tsunamis to twisters, are recorded every year. Yet over a quarter of a century, the numbers remain consistent. So why do we hold the impression that calamities are on the increase?

## In harm's way

Much of our Earth is either too cold or dry to sustain human life, so we congregate in a relatively small area. But as the population mushrooms and spreads, we consequently increase our vulnerability. With the aid of technology, we can reduce the risk from an El Nino, flood and drought. But the stakes get higher with every generation. Los Angeles, sprawled across the San Andreas fault, or the populations of the flood plains of Bangladesh, highlight this perfectly. A tectonic 'judder' can flatten a metropolis in an instant. Floods and cyclones can create famine for a quarter of a million people. By ignoring the warning signs altogether, China set a world record in 1976. The death toll from the Tangshan earthquake skyrocketed to 655,000 people. Since then, seismic observation has become a national priority. Up in the grandstand of space, these natural phenomena can be recognised for what they are. The consistent ebb and flow of the processes of a living entity. The only chaos that reigns is of our

Bush fires on the Savanna, cleanse and renew vegetation.

In Bangladesh, floods and cyclones can create famine for a quarter of a million people.

# ome

In 2 minutes a superheated gas cloud from Mont Pelee, Martinique, consumed 30,000 people.

Witness the awesome destruction of a twister.
Remember why the past is the key to the future.

## Civilised murder

In 1348 a flea found fame as a mass murderer. The Black Death or bubonic plague slaughtered almost half the population of Europe through bacteria carried by rat fleas. Millions more fell to the Spanish Flu epidemic in 1918 than in the whole of the First World War. Poor sanitation, undernourishment, ignorance and densely populated areas prove a deadly breeding ground for spreading disease even today. Our creative endeavours can be lethal, too. When a volcano pollutes the atmosphere with noxious gas, the impact is isolated. In contrast, emissions from manufacturing and transport where people live are both concentrated and continuous. The ozone layer can vouch for that. In the shadow of Chernobyl, our search for more energy has brought us to the brink of Armageddon. Yet for some, the climate remains more awesome.

## Greatest show on Earth

On Tuesday May 4 1999 Oklahoma felt the effects of a dynamic climate. And it turned their homes to matchsticks. 3 dozen twisters uprooted homes and railroad cars in a swathe of destruction half a mile wide. It was simply a clash between warm moist air and a cool dry breeze. But it turned an upcurrent into a giant vacuum cleaner. From the ringside seat of space, an astronaut is the most privileged person in the human race. Who else do you know enjoys Earth's daily command performance? For them the constant displays of lightning and the swirling cloud masses blanketing continents, signal the agents of change at work. Rainfall, wind, tides and climate shape the landscape, determine the seasons and feed the soils. Facing a twister or watching the clifftop near your home fall into the sea through coastal erosion can make it difficult to appreciate the bigger picture. Bush fires on the Savanna, for instance, cleanse and renew vegetation, while keeping the rainforest at bay. So why must we appreciate our unique relationship with Nature?

## Home sweet home

We simply can't survive on our own. We need the Earth's natural resources to sustain and nourish future generations. And as you've seen, they're all the product of billions of years of change. The environment. Food. Shelter. Doesn't it makes sense to cherish our inheritance rather than squander and exploit it? Particularly as there's nowhere else in the universe with the 'Goldilocks' factor. So the more we learn from it, the better we can learn to live with it. Blessed with an enquiring mind and a talent for tools, we're the only species capable of doing so. Who knows, one day soon, we may need our gift for technology to divert a domesday asteroid and the threat of imminent extinction. So amidst all this risk and uncertainty, what can we be sure of? That we need our dynamic Earth, more than it needs us. Because through evolution, Darwin showed us that nature simply moves on.

## Silent witness

So the next time you pick up a pebble, don't carelessly cast it away. It's really a page in a book. Earth's autobiography. If you fancy an engrossing read, there's no better place to start than at the beginning. Well, almost. Arthur's Seat and the crags are expecting you.

Round-the-clock tracking keeps a wary eye out for that domesday asteroid.

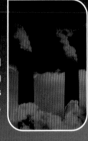

Concentrated and sustained manufacturing and transport emissions pollute our atmosphere.

If you'd like to continue your journey of discovery, here's a list of source material which will enable you to delve more deeply into the fascinating processes which have shaped our dynamic Earth.

## Series

- 'Earth Story – the shaping of our world'.
  Simon Lamb & David Sington. BBC Books.

- 'A landscape fashioned by Geology'.
  Alan McKirdy, Series Editor. Scottish National Heritage.

- Dorling Kindersley Eyewitness Guides.

## Popular Science

- 'Hidden Landscapes'.
  Richard Fortey. (Jonathan Cape)

- 'Life on Earth'.
  David Attenborough. (Collins / BBC Books)

- 'Life in the freezer – a natural history of the Antarctic'.
  Alistair Fothergill. (BBC Books)

- 'New views on old planets'.
  Tjeered van Andel. (Cambridge University Press)

www.sat.dundee.ac.uk
(Dundee Satellite Receiving Station)

www.earthcentre.org.uk
(Earth Centre)

www.esrin.esa.it
(European Space Agency)

www.geolsoc.org.uk
(Geological Society)

www.meto.govt.uk
(Met Office)

www.nhm.ac.uk
(Natural History Museum, London)

www.nssc.co.uk
(National Space Science Centre)

www.earthlines.com/rockwatch
(Rockwatch)

www.rbge.org.uk
(Royal Botanic Garden Edinburgh)

www.rgs.org.uk
(Royal Geographical Society)

# how to find

- 'Planet Earth – Volcano'.
  George G. Daniels. (Time Life Books)

- 'Meteorites'.
  Robert Hutchinson & Andrew Graham. (Natural History Museum)

- 'Realms of the Sea'.
  Kenneth Brower (National Geographic Society)

- 'Restless Earth – Nature's awesome powers'.
  H. de Blij and others. (National Geographic Society)

- 'Song of the Dodo'.
  David Quammen. (Hutchinson)

- 'Volcanoes'.
  Susanna Van Rose. (Natural History Museum)

## Recommended websites

If you have enjoyed this guide, why not visit our exciting, interactive website at www.dynamicearth.co.uk

UK
www.bbc.co.uk
(BBC)

www.bgs.ac.uk
(British Geological Survey)

www.nerc-bas.ac.uk
(British Antarctic Survey)

www.ed.ac.uk
(University of Edinburgh)

www.geo.ed.ac.uk/rsgs
(Royal Scottish Geographical Society)

www.ma.hw.ac.uk/rse
(Royal Society of Edinburgh)

www.edinburghzoo.org.uk
(Royal Zoological Society of Scotland)

www.snh.org.uk
(Scottish Natural Heritage)

USA
www.challenger.org
(Challenger Centre for Space Science Education)

www.nasa.gov
(NASA)

www.nationalgeographic.com
(National Geographic Society)

www.smithsonian.org
(Smithsonian Institute)

www.usgs.gov
(US Geological Survey)

## CD-Rom Interactive

- 'David Attenborough'.
  (BBC)

- 'Virtual Antarctica'.
  (Terraquest Adventure Series)

out more

"Go to the mountains to read the immeasurable course of time that must have flowed during those amazing operations."

James Hutton (1726 – 1797) The 'Father of Modern Geology'.